Bits and Pieces Set Aside

poems by

Judy Hoyer

Finishing Line Press
Georgetown, Kentucky

Bits and Pieces Set Aside

Copyright © 2017 by Judy Hoyer
ISBN 978-1-63534-161-4 First Edition
All rights reserved under International and Pan-American Copyright Conventions.
No part of this book may be reproduced in any manner whatsoever without written permission from the publisher, except in the case of brief quotations embodied in critical articles and reviews.

ACKNOWLEDGMENTS

Grateful acknowledgement is given to the editors of the following publications in which these poems first appeared:

Avocet: "Low Tide"
Boston Literary Magazine: "Colony Apartments"
Loch Raven Review: "The Moulin Rouge," "Rewind," "At the Shore" and "Womankind"
Main Street Rag: "The Elephant"
Naugatuck River Review: "After the War"
PMS poemmemoirstory: "Folding Sheets"
Off the Coast: "Eight Miles"
Pudding Magazine: "Love" and "My Father's Cousin"
Skylight 47: (Irish) "Spring Cleaning"
Small Portions Journal: "All I Want"
Spillway Magazine: "Seasons of Melancholy"
Surrounded: Living With Islands, an anthology of poems: "Day Trip to Block Island"
The Worcester Review: "Table" and "Winter at Bonnet Shores"
Yale Journal for Humanities in Medicine: "Cancer," "Quarantine" and "Hello"

Publisher: Leah Maines

Editor: Christen Kincaid

Cover Art: Judy Hoyer

Author Photo: Richard Hoyer

Cover Design: Elizabeth Maines McCleavy

Printed in the USA on acid-free paper.
Order online: www.finishinglinepress.com
also available on amazon.com

Author inquiries and mail orders:
Finishing Line Press
P. O. Box 1626
Georgetown, Kentucky 40324
U. S. A.

Table of Contents

When Will You Come Home? 1
All I Want 2
On This Short Dark Day 3
Destiny 5
Spring Cleaning 6
A Blessing for Grandsons 7
Grandsons 8
Birthday 9
The Moulin Rouge 10
Folding Sheets 11
After the War 12
Cancer 13
Quarantine 14
Hello 15
Last Week in December 16
Elephant 17
My Father's Cousin 18
Colony Apartments 19
Winter at Bonnet Shores 20
In the Name of Rain 21
Rewind 22
Eight Miles 23
At the Shore 25
Low Tide 26
Day Trip to Block Island 27
Womankind 29
Love 30
Seasons of Melancholy 31
Something about Summer 32
Table 33

When Will You Come Home?

Because I might die on a Tuesday sometime soon
I will go out at midnight and listen harder
than I ever have before for those two owls who
call and respond from the rafters of the oaks.

Because you are not here tonight I will make an
inventory of the way you look and bedeck the chest
of the spruce with your cheekbones, the smell of your
sweat after you've been trimming the cypress shrubs,
your razor, the cleft in your chin, the timbre of your
voice that bespeaks the mettle of the man I know.

Because I am alone the stars will brush my skin,
while across the street a family's tomorrow
is on its side like a bicycle left out in the rain.
My neighbor is queasy about yesterday's scan and fears
that she will soon alight on a branch in the sky
where the owls watch and know more than anyone.

All I Want

is to shave the essence of you
into wooden curls and fill crystal bowls with them
I know you think I'm crazy when I tell you
that it breaks out with *Blue Bayou* every time
I touch your cheekbones or the backs of your splendid hands
One spring I saw it drip from the oars you were holding
as we slid over the Concord River
My fingertip zigzags over the world map of it
from the ferryboat we took to cross the Bosporus
to the April day when hailstones filled the courtyard of Versailles
to the log cabin we rented on a paper trail in Narragansett
to the fish joint in Key Largo with the gibbering parrot
When I hear a bit of it fall on the tile floor
I bend and find it, nestle it in my palm
If you show me where you keep the Phillip's screwdrivers
I will use the right one to tighten it in place
It is the solution for anything that annoys me
burned scones, computer glitches, frozen pipes
There when coffee grounds are too difficult to explain
There between the ribs of a Dylan song that sizzles on the grill
when you turn it over with the long-handled spatula

On This Short Dark Day

It just caves in, the day that is;
an underdone cake
with scum on the blade.

My son's Saturday beard
vibrates with uncertainty
about whether to sign a lease
on the pricey attic apartment
that has no washer or dryer
as our chopsticks take turns
listening to each other's words
at the Taipei Gourmet
where the rice arrives too late.

At a quick stop for gas he realizes
the need to track back
for his wallet's absent plastic.

While I wait in the car
robins grind their teeth.
Winter moths camp in headlights.

I crack open my fortune
*Mutual assistance in despair
makes an difficult situation fair.*

Now a dash to catch a flight
to visit his twin brother in Portland
is hampered by holiday gridlock.

Taillights freeze on Route 93.
His Waze App's alternate route
waves us past a three decker
with a Nativity scene out front.

He hops out at JetBlue.
In my car's trunk are take-out boxes
stuffed with sweet and sour thoughts
of a Christmas without him.

Destiny

Like discarded mirrors, Gullah headstones
        lie cracked across the chiseled names
of Riley and Harrison
        natives who fled from dead
on god-blue currents
        to a place of unbroken happiness.
A wedding tent arrives by barge
        and anchors itself in island grass.
Clean stars align like musical notes.
        Saturday's fever loses its grip and metal chairs
find themselves sopping in dew.
        The generation that follows X
collects on a portable dance floor
        called there by the opium
of all that fat jazz and woodwind
        ferried over from a Charleston hot spot.
Three hundred arms plunge elbow deep
        into the night that stretches tight with sticky promise.
A riot of skinny straps, toned muscles
        and the good juju of a beer-can-tangle
coiled around the bumper of the couple's golf cart.

Spring Cleaning

Fill an eye-dropper with horizon and flood the holy water font.
Yank melancholy off hangers and pack in the attic with bubble-wrap.
Insist on power-washing the particles at the end of the universe.
Hold impediments up to the light like old Kodachrome slides;
discard them one by one like wild birds papered on parlor walls.
Disturb the *feng shui* of the calico cat and plaid dog.
Select three blue iris to pose naked in the privacy of the copper bowl.
Leave the south-facing door open to jugglers and acrobats.
Do what words cannot.

A Blessing for Grandsons

Bless bodies comatose that breathe in incandescent light.

Bless feet that scuttle across cold floors before skies blue.

Bless nibbles of raisin & peanut bait on plastic plates.

Bless the tense thrill of tailing a stench to its whiskered source.

Bless toy pensioners who choose elastic waists, ease-on Crocs.

Bless army men who launch stone grenades that pock pond water.

Bless things that stick, things that peel or break, cushions flying, orange flakes, duct tape swords & cardboard shields.

Bless rogue knights who urge-on cemetery steeds.

Bless the lichen they pick from their hides on a battlefield abloom with Old Glories.

Bless William who faces a concrete Christ and asks, *Is God buried here?*

Bless the little one who is pushed off the sofa and cradles an egg on his forehead the size of Humpty Dumpty.

Bless the culprit who consoles, *Don't worry Henry, you'll see Mummy yesterday, the day that has not come.*

Grandsons

Heedless sons of kings whose crowns are worn off-kilter.
Gallant sparks whose work is building towers that totter and tilt.
Thieves who sneak bites of beer and order squares of cheese.
Unbound, unbroken lords who issue decrees and thwart urgent pleas to please.
Knights whose masks clank shut in front of sharp question marks.
Spring saplings whose kingdom is covered in bark.
Unholy rulers whose verdicts are always right.
Naked, water-happy heathens who bathe in a porcelain rite.
Sires who thrust fists into the jowls of collared beasts.
Caped aces who fly over bulkheads in singular leaps.
Barefaced heirs catapulted from the Cliffs of Moher
with exaggerated tales of a never before.

Birthday

So singular is twinning!
The shock of it. The tandem pair of new.

No image of the other you.
Strapping and flimsy; one by one and double-binding.

Swinging in the feathered arms of owling.
Ripe and ready-sized. Eyes pried-blue.

What ample breath. The purse of two hearts
Pulsing in a couple-cribbed beginning.

My challenge, my fame.
Your twice-down bearing.

First one, then your brother's bottom breech.
Jousting for position from the starting point.

The jutting, jabbing joints of each.
A sizzling match : Sparks opposing.

Awkward-handed mates, counterparts who reach
Out to the other portion for the measure that's missing.

Now you are full grown, so good, so true.
Living your lives on opposite coasts. A toast to you.

The Moulin Rouge

As I spoon oatmeal
with brown sugar
and cranberries
into Henry's mouth
I am distracted
by a flashy hummingbird revue
on the patio—
a spirited can-can
with petticoats that bustle.
The troupe rustles
fruit flies nesting
on a speckled banana
that teases in orange mesh—
like a follies coquette
in fish-net hose
who draws hollers
from gents
in the front rows.

Folding Sheets

I do remember
folding sheets with her
winter stiff from the line.
She held two corners.
I knelt and found mine.
We stretched it tight.
The sounds were flitter and flap.
She was my opposite, my mother.
We brought the ends together
and pulled again.
I stepped toward her.
She took the sheet
pinned it under her chin
and brought the bottom up
to meet the top
a kind of curtsy.
It never got better than that.

After the War

Everything happened, "after the war."
White shirts were worn twice and starched for a quarter
by a tall Chinese GI who handed me a red ticket

between his wrinkled thumb and finger.
Sun shone through glass jars Papa filled with colored water
and set on the cellar window sill.

Backyard daffodils gathered in bunches
to hear him recite Wordsworth in a short-sleeved shirt.
Each morning he'd lean over the bathroom sink

and cover his face with a hot, soapy Turkish cloth
then brush on Old Spice from a glass mug.
We scoffed at Papa's warm green beans with milk and butter.

H.C. '31 vanity plates tailed the Buick up to Hanover
where he bought a bag of peanuts
and cheered the underdogs from Fitton Field.

Sunny February days, he'd be laid out
in the back bedroom, window open
hands resting empty on his chest.

Red Sox radio was his portable politics.
Never said "shit", couldn't get him to.
Never wore a wedding ring; men didn't then.

Hung hanks of tinsel on the Christmas tree one strand at a time.
Sucked brown, horehound drops that dissolved on his dentures.
At the end he could see the speck of a sailboat out in the bay

but not our faces in front of him.
On his dresser, a pair of cufflinks, a Hamilton watch
and three peeling Polaroid shots—us smiling up at him.

Cancer

Cancer is the memory of
a startled mouse traveling the perimeter
of a crowded hospital waiting room
trying to nose his way home

a young oncologist, an English major
who reads good fiction, quotes black statistics
and is right about 33% of the time

a cartoon get-well card
sent by a serious librarian famous for
scolding noisy readers that says
"It's just a bump in the road"

a neighbor's gift of Bewley's Irish Tea
bought on Grafton St. Dublin
brewed black and poured into a porcelain cup
with tiny pink roses on the rim

and a faded, finger length reminder
stitched with the skill of an Amish quilter

Quarantine

The memory burns
like scarlet fever.
I lie in a glass tableau.
No sound but
the swish of feet
under the hospital sheet.

My little brother waves
from the lawn below
my open window.
Arms aren't long enough
for us to touch.

Cards made with fat school
crayons arrive from:

Holly, who is an only child
Arthur, who sneezes when lilacs bloom
Wayne, who always wears a Cub Scout uniform
Stephen, who lives with his grandmother

Finally the fever
sheds its skin.

A nurse named Rose
helps with my clothes.
She pushes me in a
wooden wheelchair
through swinging doors.

My bride doll
is sent to the furnace
in her crinoline and lace.

Hello

Hello, she answers.
I hear the TV Mass in the background.

The nurse just left.
My 92 year old mother gets a weekly
Procrit shot for Chronic Leukemia.

"Gwen is pregnant," I tell her.
That's wonderful!

Did you know Bill Quinn?
He dropped dead.
He was the last of ten.

Last Week in December

It was after the best two days we ever had with you. Holding my cell phone to your ear while you were propped-up in your hospital bed, you told Betty, Eleanor, Virginia and Dot, *I'm dying. I don't want visitors. Good-bye.* They were all at home to take your call, except Barbara. She would remove the Telegram from its plastic sheath and turn to the obituaries. With an index finger running down the list she'd stop at her friend's name and burst out, *Jesus, Mary and Joseph!*

You insisted that Suzanne have the Oriental rug. You joked with Dick about a brief stay in purgatory. You made it clear that your war with Marjorie would continue to burn in another galaxy.

That was after we saw you in the ICU, the glass room where we played parts in a daft Irish nativity scene. You told each of us *I love you* for the first time while we breathed over you—our last Christmas together. Completing the tableau was a crystal rosary that showered its hail of beads against the metal bedside rail as you tried to raise yourself and an itinerant priest stood by holding a travel-sized jar of holy oil with both hands.

That was after the intern in scrubs steadied the clipboard so you could sign your name for the last time permitting the on-call surgeon to nail your fractured hip. It happened after you slipped on the bathroom floor in your apartment that always smelled of mothballs.

It has been a year since you died and I have placed the one thing I want to keep in an Art Deco frame. You'd like it. The picture is you at sixteen before you became my mother. You look at ease and invincible in a slim dress with a stripe running down the front.

Elephant

Marge has end-stage dementia.
The cold squash on her dinner plate

is the exact shape of an elephant's eye.
Will peace shamble in when she's asleep

in a wheelchair, her head on her chin?
Will it come when I'm asleep or when

I'm eating strawberries on the waterfront?
It could happen when Henry is painting

lurid butterflies in his cheery pre-school class,
during a terrible downpour or when I'm

on a JetBlue flight to Portland, Oregon.
The doctor said that *her body functions*

*well and it could go on and on and on
and on.* I know that we'll both be

light-hearted, Marge and me, when
it's her turn to enter a cloudless sanctuary

where miracles happen and easy chairs
have puffy legs and huge gray ears.

My Father's Cousin

The convent whisked her away
    on a Greyhound Bus.
A nightgown, comb
    and rosary beads
lay in a cardboard box
    on her lap.
My mother said
    they robbed her.
She was an English major
    a classical pianist
who lived out her days
    in a cold water flat
on Chatham Street
    next to St. Paul's Cathedral.
A card came on my birthday
    every year from "Mary."
Inside the envelope
    a crocheted handkerchief.
Sometimes I'd see her
    walking along Main Street.
She'd approach
    and murmur "Hello, Dear."
I sensed that if she spoke
    with too much conviction
she would break apart—
    a piano wheeled off a celestial
balcony onto the sidewalk
    in front of Denholms Department Store.
Felt hammers, black & white keys,
    steel strings and walnut legs
trying valiantly to piece together
    Mozart's Mass in C Minor.

Colony Apartments

The leopard-spotted cane
lies taut against the dining table
ready to pounce on a plate of bacon quiche.
She exits the room on an imaginary catwalk
with the grace of a woman who learned
to walk with Dickens on her head.
And the clock begins to tick again.

Her apartment—a replica of a
mahogany stateroom on the Queen Mary.
A lavender orchid plant with a
dozen bowing buds sucks on an ice cube.
At a family reunion atop a Sheraton end table
silver frames tell raucous stories
of fey Uncle Dan and his dog Tippy.
Philadelphia silk evening dresses (that still fit)
lie drowsing in a bottom drawer.

She stands on the balcony
looking into a cooling, custard sun.
Beyond the privet hedge
that conceals a rock garden,
beyond everything,
sits the colonial house she owned
like a yellow layer cake with
shiny chocolate frosting.
Enough room on top to light
a forest of candles.

Winter at Bonnet Shores

The swans are gone from briny Wesquage Pond.
Warm loaves of dune become the *pain perdu* of autumn

and smoky days are thin and bent.
Along the sandy selvage, camped in rows

sea roses chew the marrow of their achy joints.
Their fruit so orange, sweet and stewed.

The leaves a shock of yellow on the street.
Near granite rocks at Bonnet Point

a tire without its rim, an eel without its skin
now rest in piles of stinking algae

raked by angels fallen undersea.
An acrobatic gull scratches an absent ear

still managing to keep his perfect pose.
A sallow moon follows our car back home.

We clean the grate and build a fire of broken cedar posts.
Bloated sparks snap their fingers in our faces.

In the Name of Rain

September rain, pour down on us
Soak our quirky asylum by the Bay
With its log cabins and paper roads
Lost under poke weed and grape vines
The gray shingled houses, the bungalows
The raised ranches and the Quonset huts

Pour down on our house on Treasure Road
With the attic that kept a seaman's books
I stacked in twos and wrapped in twine
To stop the doors from slamming shut
The shelves that were lined with unsettling news
Slung on the porch by a driver from the Journal

Pour down on the house on the cliff
With the bayberry and cotoneaster shrubs
That were never supposed to lose their grip
The living room with the mismatched floorboards
Where I stood to take the call from my dying mother-in-law
Who wanted only to see *the kiddo*s one last time

Pour down on the swans, the sea grass
The groundhog who sleeps under the tool shed
The harbor seals who know when to come and when to leave

Rewind

In a beach house by the seesaw sparkle of the sea
I settle in to the day in June when the highway south
was a wide puddle of sun.
I was hit from behind.
If there was sound I did not hear it.
The car skidded sideways across the road.
I was lifted off the ground like a piece of luggage
until the car touched down in a swath of spiky grass.
Would they turn off the crock-pot?
Who would pick-up Suzanne at school?
Time stuck like pine sap on the windshield.
I was left behind as traffic whooshed by
and the car shuddered at my side.

Eight Miles

The car eases east onto Route 30.
A pop-up village opens
with whiffs of gasoline
diesel fuel, pepperoni
and scratch tickets.
A coffee chain doles out
cardboard jolts across from
Carpenter's Dairy Farm
gone to affordable housing
years ago.
I remember buying milk
that sloshed onto
the floorboards of the '76 Volare.
Dick took the car apart
on the front lawn
hosed it down with laundry soap
to get the reek of Holstein out.
Fort God staked itself
in a cornfield overnight
a big-box church
where single moms from out of town
come to pray their kids
stop with the "F" word.
The middle school across the brook
is where road-kill muskrats
find their way
into the freezer after 3p.m.
Dow Chemical, cancelled and clean
is reported to become
a hockey rink real soon.
At the intersection
of booze and double homicide
cars play a dicey game

of cat and mouse.
Wobbly telephone poles
balance trays of sky
on limbless bodies and
the Mass Pike zithers along
the road's sore back.

At the Shore

It's past the time of half and half
when night's thumbs smudge
the margins of yellowing days.
The fingers of trees
are being sucked clean.
Election posters grow on lawns—
garish, gangly perennials.
Welch—Craven—Ehrhardt
Florida license plates are scarce.
There is enough blue sky
to whiten Monday's laundry line.
Lawnmower blades are lowered.
Dogs on leashes are allowed
to run on sandy beaches.
Sweaters are still packed away.
School buses squeal the time.

Low Tide

The Atlantic
evicted on a six hour notice
has left a Nor'easter of sand
on this crescent strand
sucking cavities of crusty bones
skinning granite knees
as she turns in a rush to leave.
Hunched-back children
frantically find hermit crabs
left behind in pools of tepid brine
and lay them in colored pails
like candy Easter eggs.
Reels of lacey seaweed
trim the bonnet of the beach.
A marooned starfish sleeps
on the particles of time.
A marauding gull
craws a thick quahog—
his first catch of the day.
Sandpipers skitter
on top of shadow feet.
Their tender soles singed
on a skillet of spattering sand.
A priest-like fellow blesses the beach
with a metal detector rich on the
coins and bracelets of strangers.
A red pail lies on its side spitting salt—
the cast-off of a smooth-cheeked deserter.
The new tide moves.

Day Trip to Block Island

A horn bellows our leaving
and we ferry away from
the village of clam shacks
bric-a-brac, lobster traps, bike racks.
A woman with a kerchief on her head
cleaning plastic summer chairs
looks up as we pass her yard.
A boy stands on toothy rocks
signaling a semaphore with a stick.
He catches my eye. I wave, "Hello!"
The diesel hum muffles chatter
except for a fellow who hollers
"Sand eels are THIS big!"
Clouds are borrowed
From a canvas of *Narragansett*
by John Frederick Kensett.
I spy a silver fish swim forth
through the painterly sky
on its way up North.
Near enough, I hear
two women head to head
"Now Jean has a good thing…
She met a guy…the right address…
What a mess…I'm so depressed."
The ship's mascot, Cooper,
a barrel-built bulldog,
handsome, young, smug-mugged
seems fed-up with the voyage.
We pass Cow Cove, Clayhead.
Old Harbor's in view.
The *National* still stands—
a four-tiered white belle
with black lace and widow's walk—
stale, starched, confident.
Cars zoom out of the hold.
Couples with bikes are ready to tour.

Some with maps are ready to explore.
They know exactly what they want.

Womankind

After a mouthful
of absence
a friend's
lips stick to mine.

The wax seal
forms a bond
that's hard
to tamper with.

This is how I see it:
a bird
feeding affection
to her image
in the glass.

Love

A classic Original cylinder of Chap Stick
is rolled into place on his nightstand.

Two, sugarless Hall's Lozenges camp silently
next to a squeeze bottle of CVS nasal spray.

A single sheet of Kleenex rises from its box.
All prepared for C shift duty.

When called upon, a gunmetal-colored shoe-horn
stamped Barrie Booters New Haven & Hartford

will slip into the heels of Kiwi-polished
cordovan loafers stamped Made in USA.

His reliable Reagan-era clock radio signals 22:18.
When he finally retires in his Brooks Brothers

navy blue & red striped pajamas with the
drawstring waist, I will be asleep.

Seasons of Melancholy

dark matter too small to be stabbed with a toothpick
sadness that does not require a handkerchief

kept in a drawer with the beaded handbag
grandmother brought to her prom

there with cufflinks, pocket watches, a single lapis earring
things nobody wants

a legacy of obsolescence on mother's side
that knocks against the surface of jointed boxes

like a compendium of loose secrets
something to look back to—melancholy history

nothing to save up for
so to alleviate tip a lampshade and whisper in its ear

it's time to disappear or

strike a match and see how long flame takes to reach your fingers
know it will happen to you

Something about Summer

On a road whose name was taken from the Indians
Evening is already ankle deep—here
Where houses stand an inch above the sea
Women wait in line to buy one day at a time.

Evening is already ankle deep
And there can be no begging to be young.
Old women are grateful to pencil-in one day at a time.
They know that men are always so late.

Day darkens and the exhaust of little ones fills every room
In a beach house where hours stack like oval dinner plates
Men come home much too late to hear the
Raid of winged cicadas belting out their songs of lust.

Hours stack like stoneware bought in a musty warren of bric-a-brac.
No chance of snatching passion on a borrowed beach tonight
Where winged cicadas can be heard belting out their songs of lust
And the resident Labrador loses the groundhog chase.

No chance of passion on a borrowed beach tonight as
Blue-cheeked hydrangea raise their chins an inch above the sea
In a yard where the groundhog sleeps the stars away, on once-woodland
Where distant Narragansett hands turned branches into campfires.

Table

Our palms consider these planks of reclaimed pine
from some reluctant barn up north—Vermont perhaps.
The whorls are farmers' thumbprints
larded with a history of oats, tobacco juice
bubbling breakfast pie and the open pages
of the Bellows Falls Gazette.

We lean against the thick, live-edges.
Family furled in the corn silk of a scooped-out week.
Here to chomp on the poison ivy ropes of a boy's cliff-climb.
Gulp soft days at the arcade where tokens
Twist the neon tongues of Space Invaders.
Slurp summer jobs stripping native ears or
sliding lemon quenchers across a counter of stainless steel.

A harvest of beach stones spills across the boards.
We pick the rock printed with our names in Magic Marker.
Talismans to claim our places
and secure the flock of paper napkin birds.

I have been fortunate to be part of exceptional poetry workshops in Massachusetts, Vermont and Rhode Island. These include the Wayland, Massachusetts Public Library poetry workshop under the direction of Joan Kimball, the Colrain Poetry Manuscript Conference founded and run by Joan Houlihan which was held in Vermont, the Framingham, Massachusetts Public Library poetry workshops led by Alan Feldman, and the annual Ocean State Writers' Conference which is sponsored by the University of Rhode Island. Most of all, I am indebted to Tom Daley, a gifted teacher and poet whose classes I have taken through the Lexington, Massachusetts Community Education program and the poetry workshops that Tom runs in Cambridge, Massachusetts. I am grateful to all of you for your friendship, generosity and insightful remarks that have helped me grow as a poet. Thanks also to my family who have been so supportive along the way. This book is for you.

www.ingramcontent.com/pod-product-compliance
Lightning Source LLC
LaVergne TN
LVHW041600070426
835507LV00011B/1203